A GIFT FOR

_____

FROM

_____

BOB RECCORD
AND
RANDY SINGER

LIVE
YOUR PASSION

TELL
YOUR STORY

CHANGE
YOUR WORLD

A CHALLENGE TO FULFILL YOUR CALLING

COUNTRYMAN®

Nashville, Tennessee

Project editor: Kathy Baker

Design: Brand Navigation, LLC — DeAnna Pierce, Bill Chiaravalle, www.brandnavigation.com

Produced with the assistance of The Livingstone Corporation (www.LivingstoneCorp.com). Project staff includes Emily Malone, Paige Drygas, and Mary Horner Collins.

ISBN 1 4041 0109 8

Printed and bound in the United States of America

www.jcountryman.com

www.thomasnelson.com

CONTENTS

FOREWORDS

The prime rule of real estate is simple: "location, location, location." If you have property available in a desirable location, you have the basis for a successful transaction.

But too often we forget that the prime rule of witnessing for Christ is the same: "location, location, location." God has placed us exactly where He wants us to be, someplace we can grow and serve His kingdom, and a "successful transaction" occurs when someone receives Christ and is transformed by His power.

The book you're about to read is exciting, it's practical, and it important. Let my friends Bob Reccord and Randy Singer open your eyes to the possibilities of how you, too, can live on mission for Jesus—in your business, home, school, and community. God has work for you to do right where you are today and at every location along the journey of your life.

JENNY PRUITT
President/CEO of Jenny Pruitt & Associates, Realtors
Atlanta, Georgia

When you take a trip you need two things— a destination and a route. Those same needs apply to the journey of your life—you need a purpose and a plan!

Life is too precious a gift to be left to chance. That's why Life's Designer, Jesus Christ, has promised every one of us that He has had a purpose and plan for each of our lives from the foundation of the earth—now all we have to do is discover it, live it, and love it!

God intends for your life to be an amazing journey of faith, family, friends, work, and adventure! He designed you to change your world, grounded in the belief and conviction that God wants you to know Him personally, serve Him faithfully, and follow Him obediently. He has created you and called you to be *on mission for Him* . . . starting right where you are! It's not about what kind of position you hold . . . but rather, about what kind of perspective you have.

This book is a tool to help you examine the road map of your life's journey and to determine if you're on course. Are you headed toward the right purpose (destination) and are you following the right plan (route)? God is saying, "If you think you have a great plan for your life, *you ought to see the one I have for you!*"

So grab hold of this "travel guide" and take stock of where you're headed. It's never too late for a course correction. Perhaps you just need to pause for a breath of fresh air. Maybe you just need assurance that you're headed to the right place. And most of all, let this book remind you to enjoy the journey! After all, He created you for just that purpose.

Now, come on . . . *let's go change our world!*

JOSH McDOWELL
International Speaker and Bestselling Author
Richardson, Texas

IN ALL THE WORK YOU ARE DOING,

WORK THE BEST YOU CAN.

WORK

AS IF YOU WERE DOING IT

FOR THE LORD,

NOT FOR PEOPLE.

COLOSSIANS 3:23 (NCV)

INTRODUCTION

Regardless of age we all desperately want to leave an imprint . . . a legacy. To leave things and people better than we found them. Yet we fear that the impact of our lives could more resemble a fist in the water than a handprint in cement. The handprint is there to stay. But take the fist out of water, and for a brief moment there are ripples. Then the water settles and smoothes, as though our fist had never been there.

And so we dread the notion that, in the end, our lives might not count for much. That we might get stuck in a dead-end and thankless job that nobody notices. That our lives might be spent cleaning up the messes of others, a vicious and never-ending cycle of futility. That we might wind up as one of the "little people"— doing something mindless and meaningless.

Making life count. It's not so much about what you do as *how* you do it. And *why*.

And, most important, for *Whom* you do it.

ON MISSION:
CALLED TO MAKE A DIFFERENCE

Both of us (Bob and Randy) have looked for opportunitie
throughout our careers to tell others about our faith in Christ, what H
has done in our lives, how He has changed us, how we see Him workir
today. This deliberate and intentional sharing of our faith is what w
call being *on mission*. It's a term that encompasses more than being i
ministry—although that may be a part of it. It's a term that's broader tha
serving as a missionary—although that's also one aspect of how som
serve *on mission*. It means recognizing that the Great Commission is th
responsibility of all Christians, not just those in vocational ministry. It's
very personal awakening to a great truth of Scripture—that not only d
people in general need to know Christ, people around us need to kno
Him as well. And so *on mission* Christians look for ways to share Chris
and make an impact for Him right where we are.

THEN JESUS CAME TO THEM AND SAID,

"ALL POWER

IN HEAVEN AND ON EARTH

IS GIVEN TO ME.

SO GO AND MAKE FOLLOWERS

OF ALL PEOPLE IN THE WORLD.

BAPTIZE THEM IN THE NAME OF THE FATHER

AND THE SON AND THE HOLY SPIRIT.

TEACH THEM TO OBEY

EVERYTHING THAT I HAVE TAUGHT YOU, AND

I WILL BE WITH YOU ALWAYS,

EVEN UNTIL THE END OF THIS AGE."

MATTHEW 28:18-20 (NCV)

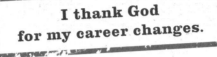

I thank God
for my career changes.

I've served in the workplace as a business executive, been a senior pastor, led interdenominationally, and presently am thrilled to be in one of North America's largest missions and ministry agencies. They've prepared me for coauthoring this book and for my position as president of NAMB (North American Mission Board). During an interview for this job, a member of the presidential search team put it this way: "In looking at your résumé, Bob, either you've made some of the dumbest career moves I've ever seen, or God has been preparing you for this role at every step of your journey." Our unpredictable twists and turns only make sense when viewed through the prism of God.

BOB RECCORD

Nobody could make a bigger career change . . .

. . . than going from a trial lawyer to a mission board employee, as anybody who knows a few good lawyer jokes can testify! Some of my partners thought I was crazy for making the move; others said they already knew I was crazy but this just confirmed it. But the most puzzling reaction came from fellow Christians who congratulated me for stepping into the ministry. "I was already in the ministry," I would tell them. "God just changed my mission field." Then they'd give me that *Are-you-serious?* look, the wheels turning. The law practice—a ministry? Our courts—a mission field? You bet!

RANDY SINGER

A HIERARCHY
OF CALLING?

Don't get us wrong. God needs more, not fewer, Christians who will respond to His high calling and go into full-time ministry. The authors of the book in your hands are leaders of a mission board. We love our jobs! And we're incredibly grateful for those who have responded to God's call on their lives to enter the mission field vocationally. They serve in the toughest places—crossing cultural, socioeconomic, and geographic barriers to reach those who otherwise might never hear the gospel. They are men and women like Dr. Taylor Fields and his wife, Susan, a gifted couple who have turned their backs on worldly success and fortune to serve inner-city kids and broken families on the Lower East Side of Manhattan. Or Sue Lowe, an eighty-eight-year-old missionary who, until very recently, went every week into the prisons of Texas, winning the most hardened convicts to the Lord Jesus Christ.

We call these folks our missionary "heroes," and we rightly honor them for the sacrifices they make in service to the kingdom. We applaud and cheer for them when they step forward and announce their intentions to follow God's call. We pray for them and support them generously with our offerings. We study the mission fields to which they have moved. But others sit slumped in their pews, feeling like second-class citizens, poor cousins to the "real" *on mission* Christians—the missionaries and the ministers.

We want to encourage the church not to send a message that elevates one type of calling while denigrating, even unintentionally, another type. And we hear from our missionaries that an unhealthy message has crept into the symbolism, terminology, and communications of the church. It's the church's own form of a caste system, and it goes something like this:

> If you're *super* spiritual and *totally* surrendered to God, you'll go to the *international* mission field.
>
> If you're *fairly* spiritual, and *somewhat* surrendered, you'll become a missionary right at *"home"*—in your own country.
>
> If you're even *a little* spiritual, yet sensitive to God's calling, then you'll at least surrender to *full-time Christian ministry* or the *pastorate*.
>
> And then, for those who want to have their cake and eat it too, you can still try *to serve God in a secular arena*—like the practice of law. (Oops . . . maybe not *that* secular of an arena!)

We hope you appreciate the tongue-in-cheek spirit in which we provide this list. Naturally, we—like our dedicated, sold-out missionary heroes—try to never propagate such attitudes. But let's be honest—some folks in the church have those attitudes, and we must be careful not to let them take root. It's our position that the church today should embrace with joy, appreciation, respect, and support not only our missionary heroes but also the *on mission* Christians who are taking a stand for Christ *right where they are.*

When Christ issued the Great Commission, He didn't emphasize the training the apostles had received, or the sermons they would preach, or the qualifications they possessed. Instead, He focused on a power that's available to everyone—from brand new Christians to seminary presidents. "But you shall receive power," Christ emphasized, "when the Holy Spirit has come upon you; and you shall be witnesses . . . "(Acts 1:8, NKJV)

The power is **universally** available. And the call is **universally** applicable.

It is also nonnegotiable. You can't hire a pastor to take your place. This is not a mercenary army. Some people will see Christ only through you. There are skills that only you bring to this great task.

So whether you are paid to be good (a full-time minister) or are good for nothing (the rest of us)—you are called to be a vital part of the Great Commission.

> You make a living by what you get.
> You make a life by what you give.
>
> WINSTON CHURCHHILL

8 PRINCIPLES
FOR FULFILLING YOUR LIFE'S CALLING

1. GOD HAS BEEN **PREPARING A UNIQUE PLAN** AND CALLING FOR YOUR LIFE SINCE BEFORE YOU WERE BORN.

2. GOD CALLS YOU TO A **LIFE-CHANGING** RELATIONSHIP WITH HIM THROUGH JESUS CHRIST.

3. GOD CALLS YOU TO **PARTNER WITH HIM** IN A LIFE-CHANGING MISSION THAT IS BIGGER THAN YOU ARE.

4. GOD REPEATEDLY WILL BRING YOU TO **CROSSROADS OF CHOICE** AS HE FORGES AND EQUIPS YOU FOR HIS MISSION.

5. GOD CALLS YOU TO BE *ON MISSION* WITH HIM **RIGHT WHERE YOU ARE**—STARTING NOW.

6. GOD REVEALS HIS MISSION THROUGH HIS WORD, HIS SPIRIT, WISE COUNSEL, AND HIS WORK IN **CIRCUMSTANCES AROUND YOU**.

7. GOD GUIDES YOU AND PROVIDES FOR YOU TO CARRY OUT YOUR MISSION **ONE STEP AT A TIME**.

8. WHEN YOU ANSWER GOD'S CALL AND FULFILL HIS MISSION, YOU WILL EXPERIENCE HIS PLEASURE AND INEVITABLY *CHANGE YOUR WORLD*.

Note: A thorough treatment of these principles appears in our book *Made to Count* and in the workbook *Made to Count Life Planner*.

L I

YOUR

LIVE
YOUR PASSION

For too long the church has left the impression that the primary place ministry and missions are accomplished is within the four walls of the church or on a foreign field totally removed from the normal traffic patterns of life. Yet Jesus spent most of His time not inside the temple, but out where the people were in life's daily tasks. And He taught those who followed Him to do the same. While He respected the temple and its purpose, He realized that the vocational priest would never get the job done alone. So He transformed tax-collectors, commercial fishermen, political activists, and a host of marketplace people. Besides, who could reach others in the marketplace of life better than those who knew it well from personal experience?

Because we're so careful to keep control over our lives, we water down the "Christian life" to the point that there is actually very little *Christ* in it. We're so concerned about it being *user-friendly, seeker-sensitive, open-minded,* and *non-offensive* that too often it can cease to be Christ-centered. In fact, if we're honest, we have to ask whether our life really reflects a commitment to a living biblical Christ or to a "cultural Christianity." We learn to go through the religious motions, use the Christian lingo, attend Christian meetings and events, but we lack the evidence of a life transformed by Jesus Christ. As Pat Morley well describes it in his book, *Man in the Mirror,* we create a god of our own preference rather than the biblical God who calls for our allegiance. We may even blame Him for the lack of fun and adventure.

Yet that's never how God meant it to be. He intended life to be an adventure . . . and to be fully and holistically integrated. God never intended to be confined to a box . . . or for any of us to be in one either. In God's view everything is sacred . . . after all, He created it all. If we're not careful, we miss the vital truth that "the only real difference between the sacred and the secular is that the secular doesn't know it's sacred yet."

The sacred was never meant to be relegated strictly to the temple or the church. Instead, the sacredness of God's mission to bring everyone into a personal relationship with Him and to become involved in His life-changing ministry to the world was intended to penetrate *every* area of life, and to involve *everyone* answering His call.

Even our Puritan forefathers got that right.

> There was for them no disjunction between the sacred and the secular; all creation, so far as they were concerned, was sacred, and all activities, of whatever kind, must be sanctified, that is, done to the glory of God . . . Seeing life whole, they integrated contemplation with action, worship with work, labour with rest, love of God with love of neighbor and of self, personal with social identity, and the wide spectrum of relational responsibilities with each other, in a thoroughly conscientious and thought-out way. . . . They were eminently balanced.[1]

When we miss this great truth, we miss out on some of the greatest opportunities for adventure life has to offer. And the Christian community, if we're not careful, lapses into a stained-glass subculture with its own music, lingo, clothing, entertainment, and business directories so that we can protect ourselves from the evils of the "world out there."

DEUTERONOMY 10:14 (NCV)
The LORD owns the world and everything in it—the heavens, even the highest heavens, are his.

DREAMS
GROW HOLY
PUT IN ACTION;
WORK
GROWS FAIR
THROUGH STARRY DREAMING,
BUT WHERE EACH FLOWS ON
UNMINGLING,
BOTH ARE FRUITLESS
AND IN VAIN

ADELAIDE ANNE PROCTER

PULLING
TEETH IN THE PULPIT

"When my oldest son was a teenager," said Richard, "God impressed on me that Brad would one day be called into the ministry. I didn't say anything to Brad, because I didn't want to put pressure on him. So I just sat back and waited to see how God would do it—in His perfect timing."

As Brad grew up, Richard, who was in full-time ministry himself, watched his son with expectant delight. God had gifted Brad with a bright mind, a love for God's Word, a desire to help God's people, and impressive speaking abilities. In addition, Brad was athletic and outgoing— someone who immediately made a great first impression. *All the skills of a successful pastor,* thought Richard. *Isn't it great to see God work!*

The years passed and Richard bit his tongue, waiting in silence as Brad announced his plans to enter the medical profession. The first year of college came and went, then the second year. *Any day now,* thought Richard, content in the knowledge that God's call is never too late. *Maybe I should say something, drop a hint, help God out a little bit.* But wisely, Richard kept his peace, waiting instead for God to call Brad in God's time and in God's own way.

The call never came. At least not the way Richard expected it.

"It wasn't until Brad got accepted into dental school," Richard told us, "that I was able to reconcile what I believe God had shown me about Brad's call into the ministry and the cold, hard fact that he was instead going to become a dentist. Suddenly, I realized that the dentist's chair would be Brad's pulpit. Then Brad went on a medical mission trip—one of the most rewarding experiences of his life—and I realized that God *had* called Brad into the ministry. Sometimes, Brad will "preach" to a captive audience in a dental chair in Atlanta, Georgia, and sometimes he will "preach" while he pulls teeth overseas. What better way to share the gospel!"

A dental chair as a pulpit! Pulling teeth as a ministry! Is this the rationalization of a demented and disappointed dad? Or is Richard onto something?

POINTS TO PONDER

1. How do you feel God can use a dentist (or a doctor, construction worker, housewife, lawyer, athlete, sales manager, and the like) to make an impact for Him in the workplace?

2. When you think of the word "vocation" what comes to mind? Look up the word in the dictionary and see if God, or divine activity, is mentioned.

3. If you're a parent, are you holding your child (regardless of age) and their future loosely . . . or striving to control and influence their direction?

4. Sons and daughters, are you listening to God's call on your life, or are you trying to live up to parental expectations?

MAKE ME
A BLESSING

An amazing thing about God's call to people throughou[t]
Scripture, and throughout history for that matter, is that He alway[s]
blessed them in order that they in turn might be a blessing. Peopl[e]
throughout Scripture were saved in order to be sent. They wer[e]
changed in order to become change agents in the lives of others. An[d]
God still works in people's lives that way.

But too often we are so focused on what we get from the gift of eterna[l]
life that we neglect what we are expected to give. There remains n[o]
doubt that salvation is a gift, but it's a gift that brings with it [a]
responsibility. That responsibility is to be involved in God's redemptiv[e]
mission to the world. God has given the ministry of reconciliation t[o]
each one who places their full weight of trust in Him. Findley Edg[e]
says it this way: "The call to salvation and the call to ministry are on[e]
and the same call." [2]

At some point we lost the sense of one's work as a calling fro[m]
God. We cheapened work by allowing it to become merely a mean[s]

earn money, acquire material goods, meet life's needs, and climb a corporate ladder. In profession after profession, job after job, workplace after workplace, men and women seem more focused on their "climb" than their "call."

As a result, guess what else has been lost: the idea of work as *divine opportunity* fleshed out in the everyday patterns of life. Divine opportunities became reserved for Sundays, religious holidays, church work or mission trips, especially for people *called* to religious service such as vocational ministry and missions.

But God never meant it to be that way. God meant our vocation to be our *platform* for making an impact for Him in the world in which He has placed us.

WORK
OR CHORES?

Renowned African-American pastor S. M. Lockeridge use to make a clear distinction between the things done *in* and *for* th church and the ministry and mission that take place *outside* th church walls. Telling of an old farmer who had his grandson visitin on the farm for a week, Lockeridge painted a poignant picture of th farmer waking his grandson for chores long before the sun rose.

Sleepy, groggy, and aching for the security of the bed's warm cover the boy toiled with his grandfather to feed the chickens, slop th pigs, water the flowers, collect the eggs, and walk the dog. He finall arrived at the kitchen where the aromas of a home-cooked farn breakfast saturated the air and greeted him.

Finishing breakfast with a slight burp, the lad felt his grandfather' hand on his shoulder and heard the words, "Let's go, boy, we've gc work to do!"

Surely, I must be dreaming, the grandson thought. "Work to do? thought that's what we've been doing!"

"No, my boy. We did chores. Anything done in the house, for the house, or around the house, . . . them's the chores. The work is what happens in the field."

Perhaps in church life, we too often confuse the chores with the work!

Ministry in the church—those are the chores. Activities at the church—ceramics classes, aerobics, fellowship times—those are not work or chores . . . they're something we want to do because those activities help us, relax us, or encourage us. But ministering and building relationships outside the church—that's the real work of a kingdom-minded body of believers!

POINTS TO PONDER

1. How are you involved in an effort to impact others for Christ outside the church walls?

2. How have you creatively found opportunity to become "the hands and feet" of Christ at your school, on your team, at work, in the neighborhood, or within your family?

FOR LOVE
OF THE AUDIENCE

Classic Greek theater revolved around three components. The *prompters* played a critical role in these live performances. They stayed down in front of the actors in an area that later would become the orchestra pit, coaching and directing the actors throughout the play. The *actors*, of course, developed the drama on the stage, hoping that the *audience* would leave pleased with the performance.

For many in today's church, those roles translate neatly into the way they view worship. The pastors, choir and praise team—those on stage—are the actors. God Himself is the prompter, orchestrating the leaders as the worship unfolds. The congregation is, of course, the audience—watching and waiting to be blessed.

Scripture teaches differently. We are told that whatever we do, we are to do it with all our hearts, as for the Lord and not for men (Colossians 3:23). Certainly this includes worship and every other activity we do associated with church. God alone is the Audience. The members are the actors, with the pastor and other leaders serving as prompters after all, the job of the leaders is not to perform, but to equip the members for the work of ministry (Ephesians 4:12).

God as Audience; members as actors; pastors as prompters. That's the blueprint Scripture gives for church. This scriptural view takes each member out of the role of critic and puts them into the role of participant. Worship no longer is viewed as a performance we judge but as an act we perform. Our question at the end of a church service should not be whether we thought the service was "good," but whether we thought God was pleased.

> So brothers and sisters, since God has shown us great mercy
> I beg you to offer your lives as a living sacrifice to him.
> Your offering must be only for God and pleasing to him,
> which is the spiritual way for you to worship.

ROMANS 12:1 (NCV)

POINTS TO PONDER

1. For whom are you living your life?

2. How does the above description alter your view
of what church should be like for you?
What difference does that perception
make Monday through Saturday?

We'll only do a few spiritual things better here on earth...

...**than we will do in heaven.** Fellowship is not one of them. Nor is worship. Neither of us authors can sing a lick here on earth (yet we know God has a sense of humor since He gave us grating singing voices to go with our musical names—Reccord and Singer). But in heaven we'll sing with the best of you.

There is *one* thing we can do now that we won't be able to do then—lead others to a personal relationship with Christ. The greatest mission of life. Sharing the best thing that ever happened to us. Helping make and develop devoted followers of Jesus Christ.

It's the most important cause we'll ever embrace.

Satan knows the battle is all about souls. If we make life easier for somebody on earth but don't ultimately change his/her eternal destiny, what does it matter? Phrased a little differently, "What will it profit a man if he gains the whole world yet loses his soul?" (Mark 8:36)

BEGIN WITH GOD,
NOT YOURSELF

Our culture consistently tells us we deserve bigger, better, pricier, and trendier stuff. And the promise is that when we get it, we'll have fulfillment. Most often we find when we arrive there, it's not nearly what we anticipated it would be.

That's because only a few things make an eternal difference—God's Word and mission, and God's people. When you combine them—fleshing out God's Word and reaching out to impact His people for His cause—**significance** results.

Go to any bookstore today and the number of self-help books will overwhelm you. Most have one focus—"You have the hidden strengths within you to accomplish everything you desire." That theme appeals to our built-in desire to be able to "do it our own way and in our own time," but although some books may offer some helpful insights, they fall desperately short: they all begin with ourselves rather than beginning *with God*. And that's a critical reversal of the proper order if you're going to live life at its best and make your life count. Certainly, we must maximize our strengths, but we must also realize that our weaknesses make room for God's power.

CRAFTED
BY OUR CREATOR

Into every life God has hardwired strengths that help each of us become unique individuals. You can see it all through Scripture.

For **Noah** there was the *tenacity* that kept him building an ark for 120 years amid the storm and ridicule of all his neighbors and despite the fact that, as far as we know, it had never rained before. (Genesis 6–8)

Abraham displayed an amazing *willingness to risk* when he left the comfort zone of one of the most advanced regions of the world to take his whole family to a destination he did not know. (Genesis 12–25)

Moses had great *courage*, whether interceding for an abused fellow Hebrew in captivity or declaring before Pharaoh, "Let my people go!" (Exodus–Deuteronomy)

Deborah demonstrated a gift for *godly counsel* as she served in a role that in many ways would be like today's military chaplains. (Judges 4–5)

David's innate *charisma* caused men to rise and follow his leadership, even in the toughest circumstances. (1 Samuel 16–1 Kings 2; 1 Chronicles 11–29)

Solomon exercised God-given *wisdom* in executing decisions that left all those around him marveling at his insight. (1 Kings 1–11; 2 Chronicles 1–9)

Esther displayed with gentle steel the *power of conviction* that saved her own people from disaster. (Esther)

Paul had a *rapier mind* that could dissect the philosophies and theologies of his day while defending the gospel of Christ. (Acts 9–Philemon)

Each of these people discovered significant God-given strengths that they used to impact their world. And each one of us is blessed with strengths of talent, intellectual capacity, physical prowess, personality skills, temperaments, and so much more—each individually crafted by our Creator for our unique lives and His purposes for us.

YOU MADE MY WHOLE BEING;
YOU FORMED ME IN MY MOTHER'S BODY.

I PRAISE YOU

BECAUSE YOU MADE ME

IN AN AMAZING AND WONDERFUL WAY.

WHAT YOU HAVE DONE IS

WONDERFUL.

I KNOW THIS VERY WELL.

YOU SAW MY BONES BEING FORMED

AS I TOOK SHAPE IN MY MOTHER'S BODY

WHEN I WAS PUT TOGETHER THERE,

ALL THE DAYS

PLANNED FOR ME WERE WRITTEN IN YOUR BOOK

BEFORE I WAS ONE DAY OLD.

PSALM 139:13–16 (NCV)

Strengths surface when we discover things we can do almost effortlessly, but which seem to be challenging to those around us. The fact that strengths are different in everybody is what makes life interesting and complementary at the same time. One person may be strong and gifted in public speaking, but absolutely despise detail planning and administration. At the same time, someone close to him may love the intricacies of strategic planning and detailed questions, but be dumbfounded at how anyone can stand up and speak or teach extemporaneously. Put them together and you will have a well-planned and orchestrated conference featuring a gifted speaker.

For that reason secure leaders learn to lead with their strengths and recruit to their weaknesses. They allow those around them to exercise their own strengths without being intimidated or threatened. In fact, secure leaders celebrate when they see teammates accomplishing great things, because they know it is a reflection on the entire team and its leadership, thus making the group far stronger than the sum of the individual members.

God gives us strengths for reasons that fit perfectly into His call and purpose for our lives.

POINTS TO PONDER

1. What are a few of the strengths that God has hard-wired into you?

2. How are you using those strengths for Him?

HUMILITY
IS THE KEY

It's amazing how God takes our strengths and weaknesse and, like clay in His hands, molds and shapes us into vessels to b used in His service. It's not one or the other, but both that make th mix unique, special, and priceless.

The balance is best achieved when we learn to live out the pictur found in John 15 of a branch abiding in the vine. It is from the vin that the branch draws its life and bears its fruit. In the same wa as we learn to depend on Christ and seek Him and His sufficienc (rather than ours), we bear fruit (make a lasting impact for Christ that endures and changes the world around us.

A key part of abiding in Christ with our mix of strengths an weaknesses is a willingness to humble ourselves before Him surrendering the strengths and acknowledging the weaknesse God tells us in His Owner's Manual that we are to submit ou selves into His hands, come near to Him, and in return He wi come near to us, day in and day out, in our living, our workin our worshiping, and our serving (James 4:7–8). Remember, God calls us to humble ourselves (so that He won't have to).

> "Humble yourselves under the mighty power of God,
> and in his good time he will honor you"

1 PETER 5:6, (NLT)

POINTS TO PONDER

1. How do you humble yourself? How are you doing in that area?

2. Would the people who know you describe you as "humble"?

3. What does humility have to do with fulfilling
   God's call on your life?

TRANSCENDING
BAD DAYS & GOOD DAYS

The plain truth is that our witness often is most powerful in the "bad days." Paul was not caught off guard by his challenges; they had been promised to him as part of his ministry (Acts 9:15–16). Today, though, we often focus on the things we must *succeed in* to make a difference, rather than the things we must *suffer through*. Our defining moments usually occur in the tough times. That's why Scripture tells us that we should "consider it pure joy whenever [we] face trials of many kinds" (James 1:2). The "rejoicing" is due to the assurance that God's at work in our lives regardless of how tough things may be. A calling transcends bad days, trials, and disappointments.

Challenges and trials refine our faith, often painfully. But prosperity is the acid test, the final exam. Prosperity is a powerful anesthesia that can deaden us to our deep, innate desire for God. Blaise Pascal observed that there's a "God-shaped vacuum in the heart of every man that cannot be filled by anything except God the Creator through His Son Jesus Christ." But we still try to fill our ives with other stuff. After all, who needs God when things are going so well?

"Give me neither poverty nor riches," says the writer of Proverbs, "but give me only my daily bread. Otherwise, I may have too much and disown you and say, 'Who is the Lord?'" (Proverbs 30:8–9, NIV)

THE PASSION

OF A YOUNG LEADER

Todd Afshar found his calling in junior high when a history teacher made current events spring to life. He started writing to congressmen and senators, and he subscribed to *Newsweek*. He started watching C-Span and CNN. During his junior year at Azusa Pacific University in Azusa, California, while studying political science, Todd decided to skip the campus politics and set his sights on higher stakes. He decided to run for mayor. Of Azusa, California. At the tender age of twenty.

The thought had first entered his mind when Todd was just a freshman. "Everybody complained about the mayor," Todd explained, "But when the elections rolled around, she ran unopposed! I decided that if she was running unopposed the next time [two years later], I would do something about it." Sure enough, after two more years of hearing complaints about the mayor, Todd heard that she was running unopposed again. His first challenge, like every politician, was fund-raising. He set a modest campaign goal of $7,000. But first, a more immediate problem. He needed $250 for a filing fee.

I just laid it all before God. 'If You want this to happen, I need the resources.' I've learned that if God calls me to something impossible, just pray for His blessing. A little while later I was standing in line at a Starbuck's. A friend's father came up and said, 'I heard you're running for mayor. I hope this helps.' When he left I reached in and opened up the check he had stuffed in my pocket. It was the exact amount I needed to enter the race."

At first, of course, nobody took him seriously. But Todd studied the issues and made his rounds. Soon, the business community started backing his fresh face. The critics raised the level of stridency—even attacking his ethnicity. Todd took it as a sign that he was no longer somebody to be laughed off. Todd and his volunteer team from Azusa put up a website, held fundraisers, registered college students, and went door-to-door.

When the votes were tallied on election day, the results were amazing: he had finished a respectable second in a three-person race, losing the election by just 700 votes. But even though he lost, Todd's passion was unfazed. He wanted to run again in 2005.

A businessman said to me that night: 'You don't realize how many walls for change you've broken down in this city.' This is what I'm passionate about. . . . Passion is something that doesn't go away. I had a bad day . . . a tough election, but I still wanted to go into politics. If I get dumped by my girlfriend, I still want to go into politics. That's my idea of a calling.

This *is* my full-time ministry. I'm not called to lead a church. I'm called to lead a city. Or maybe a nation."

Calling. The sure knowledge that God created you to do exactly what you are doing.

AN IDOL
OR A TOOL?

Sealy thought he had been called to be a lawyer. A law license became his holy grail, the practice of law his calling. He didn't yet realize that God hadn't just called Sealy to be a lawyer, he had called Sealy to be a *Christian* lawyer—the type of lawyer Jesus Christ Himself would have been if He had practiced law in twenty-first-century America. Rather than turning the law into an idol, God was calling Sealy to turn the law into a tool.

> "One week at church I learned how to share my faith actively and overtly with others. When I completed the Lay Institute for Evangelism sponsored by Campus Crusade for Christ, I was given a homework assignment. 'What we want you to do is pray about your schedule [for tomorrow] and ask the Holy Spirit to show you someone in your day that you can share the Four Spiritual Laws with. . . .'

> "The next day I had an appointment with my very first client, a referral from the Orange County Bar Association.

had worked on firm clients before, but this was the very first person coming into my office for my legal services. . . .

"After I gave her my best legal advice, I asked her if I could share something that might help her in the difficult days ahead. She immediately agreed, and I went to the other side of my desk, sat down next to her, and shared the four spiritual laws. . . .

"I do not know what happened to that woman spiritually, but I know what happened to me! Sharing the Four Spiritual Laws with her changed my life forever. My depression immediately lifted. I had finally brought God into my professional business world."

Today Sealy is a highly successful lawyer and agent. But that's not where he finds his contentment. Sharing Christ with those he meets is still the most rewarding thing that he does. That source of contentment can never be taken away. Sealy has ushered God into his daily routine and found amazing opportunities to share Christ along the way.

THE NEW
WOMAN

In today's world June Cleaver (of the *Leave It to Beaver* television series, for those of you who are too young to remember!) is a woman of the past. And we're not sure she was ever a realistic role model. What June did best was say, "Yes, dear," or "Now be patient with the Beaver, dear." And she was always smiling at the door as Ward left for work and when he came back home. Always in hose and heels, of course.

Today's woman is more colorful. She exercises skills and strengths, multiple talents and interests, and a gifted mind. Her family means everything to her, and she wants to make a difference in her world as well. She may work inside the home, outside, or both. Gone are the days when *one size fits all.*

Whether a woman finds herself in the marketplace full-time, part-time, or as a stay-at-home mom, how can she make her home a nerve center for ministry?

Christian women are amazingly creative—they find ways to make a difference without adding a lot of additional commitments to their already demanding schedules. We'll share a few of them on the next several pages to spark your imagination.

SHE IS STRONG

AND IS RESPECTED BY THE PEOPLE.

SHE LOOKS FORWARD TO THE FUTURE WITH JOY.

SHE SPEAKS WISE WORDS

AND TEACHES OTHERS TO BE KIND.

SHE WATCHES OVER

HER FAMILY AND NEVER WASTES HER TIME.

HER CHILDREN SPEAK WELL OF HER.

HER HUSBAND ALSO PRAISES HER

SAYING, "THERE ARE MANY FINE WOMEN, BUT YOU ARE

BETTER THAN ALL OF THEM."

CHARM CAN FOOL YOU, AND BEAUTY CAN TRICK YOU, BUT A

WOMAN

WHO RESPECTS THE LORD

SHOULD BE PRAISED.

GIVE HER THE REWARD SHE HAS EARNED; SHE SHOULD

BE PRAISED IN PUBLIC FOR WHAT SHE HAS DONE.

PROVERBS 31:25-31 (NCV)

A BIRTHDAY
PARTY FOR JESUS

As Christmas approached, Linda wondered how she might impact her neighborhood. She decided to get her children involved and have a "Birthday Party for Jesus." Linda and her kids worked together on the project. They designed invitations and then walked house to house in the surrounding neighborhood handing out the invitations to kids who were in their age range. As each mother came to the door, Linda explained that they were hand-delivering invitations to a very special birthday party for a very special person.

Linda was careful not to hide the intent of the party to the mothers. In fact, she explained clearly what their kids would be doing—celebrating the birth of the One who Christmas is all about by singing Christmas songs about Jesus and having a birthday cake . . . playing games such as "Pin the Tail on Mary's Donkey" . . . having an all-around blast! As the highlight, Linda would read the Christmas story from a book written in simple words about the birth of the Greatest Person who ever lived.

Mother after mother was thrilled with the idea and excited about their children going to the party. Some mothers wanted to come, too!

Linda involved her kids at every step. The kitchen was transformed into a "goody factory" as they made Goody Bags for every party-goer. And to emphasize the ultimate purpose of the gathering Linda gathered her kids around the table daily to pray for every invited child. After all, the purpose was to let them know that God loved them so much that He sent His only Son to change their lives . . . and their parents as well. Who could tell what this holiday event could accomplish!

The first party was several years ago. Linda has continued to have a birthday party for Jesus every year. It has provided numerous opportunities to share how the Guest of Honor at the party can take up residence in the hearts of the kids, and adults, who attend.

POINTS TO PONDER

1. What are some of the significant ways you have watched God use homemakers to make a difference for Him and change their world?

2. Describe the qualities you most admired in them.

3. How could you creatively use your home as a "nerve center" to impact others for Christ?

MAKING
A DIFFERENCE

Jeanine lives with her husband and two daughters in Lawrenceville, Georgia. In 1998 Jeanine learned she had breast cancer. Going through one mastectomy, she thought she had found health and a new lease on life.

And so she had . . . for a year. That's when the cancer came roaring back, and Jeanine suffered through another mastectomy, cancer found along the spine, tumor counts that resembled a roller coaster in tracking, and untold chemo and radiation treatments. But several years later, Jeanine is still valiantly fighting the battle. She is an encouragement to everybody who knows her.

Her commitment to make a difference for Christ even during the tough times led Jeanine to ask her husband, Chuck, not to accompany her when she went for her cancer treatments. When Chuck tried to resist, Jeanine would have none of it. It took her only moments to explain to Chuck that other women who were receiving cancer treatments would be much more open to talk with her and respond to her, if her husband were not there.

"I love you, honey. And I really appreciate your wanting to go with me and support me. But maybe God's allowing me to have this difficult time so that I in turn can help another who is going through the deep valley. And who knows, maybe God has a divine appointment for me while I'm sitting in a chemo treatment chair!"

And needless to say, Jeanine leaves a wake of blessing everywhere she goes as she continues to bravely fight the battle of cancer—but in the midst of it, she is *on mission* for her Master! And she does it all in the normal traffic patterns of her hectic world.

And the persons she's impacting the most? Her own family. As her girls watch their mom handle the toughest circumstances life can dish out, they are learning how to be *on mission* in the face of adversity. They are also learning first-hand how to make a home a ministry center.

It makes you stop and think doesn't it? If Jeanine could make a difference like that even in the tough days she's walking through, . . . what could God do with you?

POINTS TO PONDER

1. What's the toughest thing you're going through in your life? How does Romans 8:28 apply to you?

2. What good could come out of your challenges according to James 1: 2–3?

3. Why is it important to grab hold of the truth of 2 Corinthians 12:8–10 if you feel there's no way you can change your tough times?

IN HIS
PERFECT TIMING

God's ways (and timing) have never been synonymous with ours:

> "For My thoughts are not your thoughts, nor are your ways My
> ways, says the LORD. For as the heavens are higher than the
> earth, so are My ways higher than your ways, and My thoughts
> than your thoughts" (Isaiah 55:8-9, AMP).

God's working with His chosen nation, Israel, is an excellent example of this critical truth. After promising the land He would give them as far back as Abraham, He continually had to remind them that it was His timing, not theirs, that was essential. He waited years until He was ready to deliver them from bondage in Egypt to set out for their Promised Land. And even then He warned them not to expect a "fast fix." He reminded them of His faithfulness, but cautioned them to remember His timing as they headed for the enemy-inhabited Promised Land.

> "You may say to yourselves, 'These nations are stronger than
> we are. How can we drive them out?' But do not be afraid of
> them; remember well what the LORD your God did to Pharaoh

and all Egypt. You saw with your own eyes the great trials, the miraculous signs and wonders, the mighty hand and outstretched arm with which the LORD your God brought you out. The LORD your God will do the same to all the peoples you now fear. . . . The LORD your God will drive out those nations before you *little by little. You will not be allowed to eliminate them all at once*" (Deuteronomy 7:17–19, 22, NIV, italics ours).

They were ready to take over in one fell swoop, but God knew that for their good and the long-term effectiveness of His plan, His timing was better than theirs.

It's the same in our walk with God and being *on mission* with Him wherever He's placed us. We're ready for radical change tomorrow, with us as the catalyst, but He's looking for eternal transformation, and that takes time. **We tend to overestimate what we can accomplish in one year, but underestimate what we can accomplish, with God's blessing, in five years.**

HOW TO
LIVE YOUR PASSION

START BY WRITING DOWN THE MISSION OF YOUR OWN LIFE:

What do you believe God has called you to do?

What are some gifts and talents you have that you can use to make a difference vocationally? What about at church?

What are some gifts and talents you have that you can make a difference with as you use your home, apartment, or dorm as a ministry base?

How could your family and friends work with you?

SCHEDULE A TIME TO PRAY AND PLAN:

Begin by informally talking through some out-of-the-box thoughts of how you can use the gifts and talents you identified to accomplish your mission.

Begin with prayer asking God for wisdom and discernment.

List where your normal traffic pattern takes you throughout the day. Identify the needs you come in contact with.

Make notes of everybody's input
and then narrow down the possibilities.

Pray that God will help you when taking the first
steps in an action plan.

SET A GOAL AND MAKE IT PROMINENT:

It's easy to talk about the action plan;
it's another thing to do it. Write it down.
Putting it in print makes your dream concrete.

Make your action plan *doable, measurable,
practical, and enjoyable.*

Put it in a prominent place like a refrigerator or mirror,
or perhaps a note on the dashboard of your car.

STAY ON TRACK:

Ask your spouse, family members, or friends to hold
you accountable for the project.

Remember, you'll be tempted to overestimate
what you can accomplish in a month and
underestimate what you can accomplish in six
to twelve months. So keep the end in mind.

Ministry isn't always what we go and do.
It's what we do as we go.

NELVIN VOS

WHAT
MAKES A HERO?

Heroes, according to Webster's Dictionary, are those person
we admire for their courage and nobility. They inspire *hope, possibilitie*
and *dreams.* Everyone needs a few good heroes.

When we grew up (yes—a long time ago), heroes were plentiful on th
television on Saturday mornings. Sky King, Roy Rogers, the Lon
Ranger, and Superman flew and galloped across the screen. Each on
personified values, actions, and attitudes that set a high bar for those o
us who watched. They became models for the molding of our own cha
acter and personalities. We did what they did, or at least tried what the
tried. (That "leaping tall buildings" thing got to be a little tricky.)

ines between good guys and bad guys were clear and crisp then. For the good guys, ego-driven aggrandizement was less important than serving others. Taking credit took a back seat to deflecting credit. Truth was an ltimate goal . . . an absolute, rather than a moving target. Friendships ere valued and guarded, not disposable and inconsequential. And he heroes of yesteryear were not loved for their money but for their magnanimity. Like the bespectacled Clark Kent, the heroes were fallible nd ordinary, with an uncanny ability to always rise to the challenge. In hort, we could identify with them, not just idolize them.

Je want to introduce you to some modern heroes—ordinary people ho believe in an extraordinary God. They've discovered that . . .

Success is not as fulfilling as faithfulness.

Notoriety is not as important as integrity.

God loves you right where you are, but He loves you too much to let you stay there.

The mission of a believer's life is the Great Commission of their Savior.

The promise of Ephesians 3:20 is real—"Now glory be to God! By his mighty power at work within us, he is able to accomplish infinitely more than we would ever dare to ask or hope" (NLT).

o join us as we introduce you to some of our favorite ordinary people . . . hom God is using in extraordinary ways—*right where they are!* But on't put them on a pedestal; they don't want that. Their lives are spiring not because they have it all together, but because they point the One who does.

JESUS IN A
LAW SCHOOL PROFESSOR

Ruth discovered that she had a gift for teaching. The students were engaged by her classes and she would get consistently great reviews. We talked to students who learned from Ruth years ago and still rave about her teaching style and what a great role model she was. She has been teaching now for eleven years—a Oklahoma, with stints in between as a visiting researcher at Harvard Law School and with international institutes in Germany and Switzerland, and now at the University of Minnesota.

She believes it is important to have "believers in every sphere and ever situation." And that applies to our institutions of higher education where values are shaped and lives are molded. "It has stretched me," Ruth admits, "to be in the midst of so many nonbelievers."

She reaches her students through building wise relationships.

"I have an open door policy. And a teacher gets lots of questions 'How did you get to be a teacher? How did you decide what career path to take?' This gives me a chance to give my testimon because I'm a role model to them. If they want to know who I am, what makes me tick, I share from the Bible. I can't separate who I am from the words of Scripture. And if students have needs— I pray with them. . . . [and] I share from Scripture. There is no situation in the lives of my students that the Word doesn't have something to say about . . . I tell my students: 'I am interested in you!'"

Ruth recognizes that students respond to authenticity and love. The approach has served her well. Though highly regarded for her academic prowess and superior teaching ability, the real key to Ruth's impact on her students is that she takes time to build lasting relationships. She shows them Christ—in the form of a law school professor.

Historically the Christian community drove the arts.

Walk the halls of the Louvre in Paris and study the great works of the masters. Most of them illustrate explicitly religious themes. Consider the explosion of information facilitated by the Güttenberg Press. It was Christians who saw that tool as an amazing system to deliver the message of a loving and transforming God to a world that was dying to hear. Travel to Rome and gaze at the Sistine Chapel. Creation is depicted through one man's artistic genius, and the message of God's divine purpose is clearly evident. Travel to Florence and view the breathtaking creations of Michelangelo. Biblical characters are frozen in a snapshot of time, delicately carved out of now-weathered marble. The impact of the Christian community is ubiquitous in the history of the arts as well as the growth of communications through media.

But in today's culture, the Christian community has circled its wagons, intent on building its own culture. Christians make movies for Christians. And Christian television has little appeal for the unchurched. Too many Christian books concentrate on what can be done for the families already involved in the church and not on how to impact those outside the church with Christ's redemptive message.

NO ONE

AFTER LIGHTING A LAMP

COVERS IT WITH A BOWL OR HIDES IT UNDER A BED.

INSTEAD,

THE PERSON PUTS IT ON A LAMPSTAND

SO THOSE WHO COME IN WILL

SEE THE LIGHT.

LUKE 8:16 (NCV)

THE FIRST DEMAND

ON A CARPENTER'S RELIGION IS THAT HE MAKES

GOOD TABLES.

WHAT USE IS ANYTHING ELSE IF IN THE CENTER OF

HIS LIFE AND OCCUPATION

HE IS INSULTING GOD WITH BAD

CARPENTRY?

DOROTHY SAYERS

DOWN TO
EARTH AMONG THE STARS

Victorya Rogers has been a leading talent agent in Hollywood. As she began sharing Christ there, Victorya learned an amazing thing—people in Hollywood didn't want her to be perfect, they just wanted her to be real. The greatest opportunities to share her faith came when she showed her own vulnerabilities. Sometimes she unintentionally offended someone and had to apologize and ask for forgiveness. Other times she experienced difficulties, yet had opportunities to explain that only her relationship with Christ could get her through them. She states:

> "There are times when I want to tell God, 'I've hurt enough.' I've been stalked by a rapist; heartbroken by different experiences. I've been maliciously sued and falsely accused, and I've had disappointments at every turn. But in the very center of those challenges, I have found countless opportunities to share the difference Christ has made in me. For me, one of the key passages has been John 15:7–8. I really work hard trying to

make sure that I am confidently abiding in my relationship with Christ and that His Word abides in me."

And it must be working. Victorya is having an amazing impact in the Hollywood community. She explains her approach:

"All I have to do is share my faith with those around me who are searching. If they find Jesus, He will change their behavior, not me. That means their television programming and products eventually improve. It is humbling to think that sharing Jesus with only one person may have enough impact to change the world.

"The way I've learned to tell His story in my Hollywood environment is to first hear the story of those with whom I work, to walk alongside them and know what their lives are all about. The only way to reach people for Christ is to get involved in their lives!

"Yet Christians, in fear, keep running from Hollywood. But if we don't have Christians there, Hollywood will never change for the good. I just want every day of my life to count for eternity. I don't have the luxury of wasting any more time!"

When was the last time you prayed for Hollywood? Have you prayed for it as often as you have criticized it? Do you know someone who is leaning toward the media and arts as a career? If so, how can you be an encouragement to them? What help can you offer to equip them in their Christian walk so that they can make a difference for Christ wherever He happens to open a door for them. Maybe you're leaning toward a career in the media or arts. Are you ready to be vulnerable and minister to others through the valleys?

If God is calling you to the media or the arts, why don't you start looking for opportunities right where you are to use newspaper articles, movies, and television shows as a starting point for sharing Christ?

PROCLAIMING
THE TRUTH

Peggy Wehmeyer fell in love with Jesus, not at a "safe" place like a youth camp or retreat, but while studying at the University of Texas at Austin. She began her walk with Christ filled with anticipation, excitement, and expectancy. She wanted to make a difference! The campus ministry people around her were supportive, encouraging, and affirming. Then she decided to become involved in student government and in the journalism department. She was surprised by her friends' reaction: "You won't have enough time for ministry, and ministry has eternal significance." They thought journalism wouldn't be a good use of Peggy's time.

So began the interesting journey of a gifted young woman, thankful and thrilled to be a new Christ-follower, yet confused by some of the Christ-followers around her. Still, she clung tenaciously to her belief that Christians were to be salt and light. They were called to penetrate the culture, not shun it.

Despite the naysayers and dream crushers, Peggy's passion was undimmed. She weathered the criticism and continued to thrive in her media environment. She observes: "Journalism for me is more than the passion of loving to tell stories and communicate and write; it is pursuing the truth at all costs!" Peggy's commitment to excellence while maintaining her spiritual convictions eventually paid off—ABC headquarters invited her to be the network's religion correspondent, reporting to Peter Jennings.

Peggy also realized that modern journalism is one of the most powerful institutions in existence.

> "Our children's generation is more shaped in their thinking and values by the media than they are by the government, education, or most anything else. The media has an incredibly powerful role in shaping our culture. So if God's purpose is to bring light into the darkness, and the news is to be the greatest purveyor of 'truth,' Christians should want to have an influence there. I am committed to the fact that God has called all of us to make Him recognizable through our lives and our work, wherever He places us, and I can't personally think of a more exciting place to do that than the world of media!"

Peggy looks sadly at the perspective of so many churches that shy away from media and entertainment.

> "To me, the church has abandoned the key places of influence like Hollywood. My question is, 'Why has the church abandoned these places?' And now that the church has, it's much more difficult for Christians who do make it in those worlds to

survive there because there's not much support. So we, as Christians, are probably to blame for making the media arena such a hostile place for evangelical Christians. After all, we're the ones who left!"

Peggy's prayer for the future is that God would commission more outstanding, young Christ-followers into the profession of journalism.

"The church is way behind the game of having top-notch journalism schools. When you look at the schools where top journalists are coming from, on the East Coast for example, these are not places where the church is sending their kids. I would say we should be strengthening our journalism programs, but until they are strengthened, we should be preparing and sending young Christians to the top journalism graduate schools in America, giving them the strength to be able to stand firm once they get there. If we want to touch our world, we need to be good at what we do, and we need to use our gifts in places of influence."

Whenever there is a deep, heartfelt passion, you don't have to look far to find somebody who will try to kill it. Even well-intentioned people within the church can be quick to tell you why you shouldn't move in a direction that fits your passion. Many prefer the comfort of isolated and non-threatening environments to the challenging opportunities of stepping into an arena where, though it may be uncomfortable, you could make a significant difference.

You begin to look at people differently when you're...

... *on mission* for Christ in a challenging environment like Hollywood or the media. While it's easy to become judgmental and count people out, when you're truly *on mission* you begin to see through a different lens. You see what people can become with the impact of Christ, not just what they presently are. It's not an easy transition—but it's a critical one!

Are you expecting the unexpected in your walk with God? Are you open to new opportunities that don't necessarily fit into the "master plan" you have for your life? Are you praying for an easy path, or are you willing to walk down a tougher one that may lead to greater impact? And finally, have you lost sight of your calling, or started thinking that your time has passed you by?

Justice.

A concept precious to God and integral to His character.
"Righteousness and justice," says the psalmist, "are the foundation of [God's] throne" (Psalm 89:14, NKJV). God loves justice and hates those who pervert it (Psalm 11:7, Isaiah 61:8, Micah 3:9–12). "For the LORD is a God of justice" (Isaiah 30:18, NIV).

You would think that His followers must be taking up the cause, filling our law schools and legal profession with Christian lawyers who practice law based on the principles of Scripture.

Not so, according to Sam Casey, director of the Christian Legal Society, and a man who tracks the trends in the legal profession very closely. "According to George Barna, no more than 4 percent of lawyers are Christian in their orientation. And according to George Gallup, who is frankly a little more liberal in his definition of Christianity, no more than 10 percent of that group are Christians."

FROM THE
INSIDE OUT

"The more I saw of state politics, the more I became frustrated about what government was doing, and sometimes not doing, for the citizens and kids in schools. As my kids got to public school age, I became more and more of an activist. We passed a Human Life Amendment to the State Constitution that I was deeply involved in. I also was up to my neck in involvement with citizens against legalized lottery and an anti-gambling crusade. My experience showed me firsthand that one of the main problems we had was that most Christians were willing to stand out on the Capitol steps trying to be a voice *to* government, but very few were willing to actually get inside the Capitol with a voice *for* government. I became convinced that one of the best ways to change things was not simply from the outside shouting inward, but from the inside and working outward."

MIKE HUCKABEE
governor of Arkansas

Mike Huckabee, governor of Arkansas, is convinced that God's call is fluid and may put a person in different positions at different stages of their journey through life. The man who went from the pastorate to the governor's mansion also emphasized that *every* vocation needs Christians called to make a difference.

> "You can see it with the Biblical characters—people like Moses, Joseph, David and the Disciples. I think that every vocation should, in fact, be the result of a *call* if a person is a believer and Christ-follower. Because as people who believe in Jesus Christ, our entire lives ought to belong to Him. Not just the spiritual compartment, but all of our life should belong in His care and direction. I can't help but believe that if He's interested in healing, He will call some people to be doctors; since He's the Mighty Counselor, He would call others into counseling; as He established and created commerce, He would call still others into business as salt and light. He's going to call people wherever there's a sphere of influence, whether it be politics, playwrights and actors, medicine or any other area. And there's no greater place to be than where you know God has called you to live out your life for Him!"

SPIRITUAL
SENSITIVITY

"**When you are sensitive to God's will for your life** and you are honest before God, . . . there are some things that you're going to want to do and God's not going to want you to do them. But if you say to God, 'I'm willing to accept *whatever* Your will is,' that's when you see God move mountains. That's when you see divine intervention. The trouble people get in is we want to do things so badly and we get so emotionally involved. When the Lord says, 'No, J. C., that's not where I want you, that's not what I want you to do,' that's when I'm tempted to take out the spiritual crowbar and try to pry the door open. And when we walk through those doors, we see that God has nothing to do with it. But if you are open and sensitive to God's will for your life and you're willing to accept God's saying "yes" or "no," mighty things happen when God is in the process."

J.C. WATTS
former Oklahoma Congressman

And how do you know if God is calling you into a life of public service? Here are some insights that former Congressman J. C. Watts shared with us:

> Prayer, sincere prayer.
>
> Don't put the cart before the horse. Don't do it and then pray about it. Pray first.
>
> You have to be prepared for God to say "yes," but you have to be equally prepared for Him to say "no."
>
> If God speaks to your heart, then go forward with great gusto.
>
> Seek wise counsel from those who have done it, those who have gone before you.
>
> Make sure your spouse fully understands the sacrifices and commitments of public service.
>
> Always consider your family. Will it be a hardship for them? God will never call you to anything that will wreck your family.

POINTS TO PONDER

1. Could God be calling you to the arena of public service?

2. How could Christ use you to be *on mission* for Him in the public sector?

3. Why don't you take a moment and pray for the president, the justices of the Supreme Court, your senators, your representatives, your governor, and your mayor. And don't forget to pray that God will call many more who know Christ personally into these arenas.

OPEN
TO OPPORTUNITY

Sometimes we learn more in defeat than we do in victory.
And sometimes when a door slams shut on one opportunity it opens for
two or three others. Such is the case with Vernadette Ramirez Broyles.
We interviewed her not because she won an election, but because she
gained some valuable insights along the way that might help all of us.

Reflecting on her failed attempt to become the Secretary of State for
Georgia against a very strong incumbent, and the opportunities that
followed on the heels of that defeat, Vernadette had this to say about
lessons learned:

> "It is clear to me that God's people remain on earth in order to
> infiltrate every avenue of life, to be on *mission* for Him while
> serving others. God intended His people to be in medicine and
> government and media, and every other occupation. We're to
> be salt—a preserving element, and light—illuminating God's
> principles through practical living and showing how to know
> Him personally through practical believing.

"Because we need to infiltrate every area of life as we serve our Lord and Master, we need to understand that too often the world considers the church irrelevant, and they would prefer to marginalize us. It's much more difficult to do that when Christians are actually a part of the fabric of daily life. It is especially difficult to do it when Christians who are a part of that everyday fabric, do what they do in the marketplace, in whatever realm, with excellence and high performance . . . and you've always got to be ready for opportunities that come knocking at your door. . . . One of them that always comes knocking at my door is, 'How did you go to Yale and Harvard, coming from the Bronx in New York?' And that throws open a door to tell people just how faithful God really is and how He can work in an individual's life.

"And today, God has opened a door for me to be a national consultant in faith-based initiatives, which the President has made one of his major emphases. And still other doors to serve on the board of the Department of Human Resources for the state, as well as the governor's Latino Commission for a New Georgia. My background in politics and law, as well as my education at Yale and Harvard, have been amazing stepping-stones toward being able to bring biblical influence in ways I never dreamed possible."

For Vernadette, "opportunities" are not just about new career moves or platforms for sharing her views. "Opportunities" are more often about people and making some positive impact on the life of someone else for Christ.

Perhaps the first years of your life, or the first years of a new job or a new school or a new marriage, have been like a trip up the hill with the brakes on. Have you let that beginning be a steppingstone to help you make things better, or has it become a stumbling block, tripping you up and keeping you from answering God's call and fulfilling life's purpose? Are you running ahead of God? Are you willing to lay your hopes and dreams on the altar so you can really be certain you're following God's plan for your life and not your own?

WHEREVER YOU ARE IN THIS
JOURNEY
CALLED LIFE, WHEREVER YOU MAY BE EMPLOYED,
WHEREVER YOU MAY BE
IN YOUR DOMESTIC SITUATION, WHEREVER YOU MAY BE

IN YOUR AGE, YOUR HEALTH OR YOUR LIFESTYLE,
GOD MAY BE PREPARING YOU
FOR A GREAT SURPRISE IN ORDER TO FIND YOU
FAITHFUL.
RATHER THAN RUNNING FROM HIM,
RUN TOWARD HIM.
AND RATHER THAN LOOKING FOR SOMEONE TO BLAME

FOR THE PAIN THAT YOU'RE NOW ENDURING OR

THE CHANGE THAT'S ON THE HORIZON,
LOOK HEAVENWARD
AND REALIZE THAT THIS ARRANGEMENT

IS SOVEREIGNLY PUT TOGETHER FOR YOUR GOOD AND
FOR HIS GLORY.[3]

CHARLES SWINDOLL

"One thing I learned during my run for governor...

...was that obedience to Christ always leads to illumination of the path He wants us to walk. Illumination doesn't lead to obedience. Too many of us are waiting for the path ahead to light up before we obey what we already know. That's so fundamental! We cry out, "God, show me Your will, show me Your will, show me Your will." But what I've come to conclude is that God is perfectly willing to reveal His will if He's convinced that obedience is there. We won't lack the light we need to move ahead if we're willing to obey one step at a time. We just usually want the whole pathway lit before we obey even the first step."

SONNY PERDUE
governor of Georgia

LIVING
THE DIFFERENCE

When Bob asked Sonny how he had seen God move in and around the governor's mansion since he began inhabiting it, tears formed in his eyes.

> "As God tells us, to whom much is given, much is required. We've been afforded a great opportunity to live in this, the people's house. We have had a tremendous opportunity to unashamedly talk about our faith and the importance of faith in all people's lives regardless of their beliefs. We have also come to understand that ministry still happens one-on-one."

Sonny also shared about how those one-on-one opportunities work. One of the men working in the governor's detail began asking a lot of questions about the faith he saw and heard in the governor and his family. Helping with numerous activities, the staff member would overhear faith-oriented discussions that seemed to resonate with joy, purpose, and peace. As the questions mounted for this staff member, an opportunity came to encounter Christ's loving plan for his life right in the midst of his duties for the governor. Today, he is growing as a new Christ–follower. Many others now are asking the same questions on their own time and during personal and private conversations.

Sonny and Mary Perdue believe they have been placed in the gubernatorial role to lead the state and to represent their Lord. "As the governor and first lady we must respect the office, and at the same time we intend to live a lifestyle that will encourage people to look for what the difference is. And we will be ready to tell them the difference is Christ."

JEREMIAH 23:4 (NCV)

"I WILL PLACE NEW LEADERS

OVER MY PEOPLE, WHO WILL TAKE CARE OF THEM.

AND MY PEOPLE WILL NOT BE AFRAID

OR TERRIFIED AGAIN, AND NONE OF THEM WILL BE LOST," SAYS THE LORD.

WHEN YOU'RE FOLLOWING GOD, YOU'LL FIND NO SHORTAGE OF CRITICS AND PESSIMISTS. FOR EVERY PERSON WHO WILL AFFIRM YOUR DECISION **TO OBEY GOD'S CALL, YOU WILL FIND FIVE WHO** WILL TELL YOU WHY YOU SHOULDN'T DO IT. BEING OBEDIENT TO GOD'S CALL IS NOT A JOURNEY FOR THE WEAK-KNEED OR THE SOFTHEARTED! **ONCE YOU'VE HEARD** THE VOICE OF GOD (SEE JOHN 10), DON'T BE DISTRACTED **BY ANY OTHER VOICE, REGARDLESS OF HOW WELL-INTENTIONED.**

FAITHFUL...
NO MATTER WHAT

"Darius thought it would be a good idea to choose one hundred twenty governors who would rule his kingdom. He chose three men as supervisors over those governors, and Daniel was one of the supervisors. The supervisors were to ensure that the governors did not try to cheat the king. Daniel showed that he could do the work better than the other supervisors and governors, so the king planned to put Daniel in charge of the whole kingdom. Because of this, the other supervisors and governors tried to find reasons to accuse Daniel about his work in the government. But they could not find anything wrong with him or any reason to accuse him, because he was trustworthy and not lazy or dishonest. Finally these men said, 'We will never find any reason to accuse Daniel unless it is about the law of his God.'" —Daniel 6:1-5 (NCV)

You know the story. Daniel's jealous co-workers got the king to forbid praying to anyone except the king, Daniel prayed to God anyway, and he got thrown to the lions for his faithfulness.

"The next morning King Darius got up at dawn and hurried to the lions' den. As he came near the den, he was worried. He called out to

Daniel, 'Daniel, servant of the living God! Has your God that you always worship been able to save you from the lions?'

"Daniel answered, 'O king, live forever! My God sent his angel to close the lions' mouths. They have not hurt me, because my God knows I am innocent. I never did anything wrong to you, O king.'

"King Darius was very happy and told his servants to lift Daniel out of the lions' den. . . . Then King Darius wrote a letter to all people and all nations, to those who spoke every language in the world:

> I wish you great peace and wealth.
> I am making a new law for people in every part of my kingdom. All of you must fear and respect the God of Daniel.
> Daniel's God is the living God;
> he lives forever.
> His kingdom will never be destroyed,
> and his rule will never end. . . .

"So Daniel was successful during the time Darius was king and when Cyrus the Persian was king." —Daniel 6:19–23, 25–26, 28 (NCV)

Daniel had a prestigious job working for one of the most powerful men in the world, a man who did not share Daniel's beliefs. But Daniel's professional excellence and unwavering faith earned him such esteem that it opened the door for God to work in the lion's den, in the king's heart, and throughout the known world. Do your boss and co-workers see excellence in your life because of the way you work? In school, home, and business are you bowing to the king or to the King?

A TRACT
OF YOUR LIFE

Congressman Jim Ryun is a lifelong runner. In 1965, Jim set the male high school mile record—a mark that stood for thirty-six years. He ran in the 1964, 1968, and 1972 Olympic games, winning a silver medal in the 1500-meter run in 1968. Jim also held the world record in the mile, 1500 meters, and 880 yards, and he achieved legendary status as the first high school student ever to run a sub-four minute mile.

But there came a time when he realized there was more to life than running.

> "My wife, Anne, and I had been married for a time, and we began to realize that no amount of success in running would fill that need in our life, that only a relationship with Jesus Christ would. As we were training for the Olympics in 1972, God put in our path some Christians who simply shared that it's not religion, but having a relationship with Jesus Christ that would last, and it's not a Sunday relationship, but an everyday relationship with Him."

When Jim and Anne put their faith in Christ, that faith was soon tested. Jim fell during a qualifying race in the 1972 Olympics, taking him out of the running for Olympic gold. To complicate matters, he was sure he had been pushed. The race was on video—clear proof of how it happened. "Though the video proved I had been fouled, the Olympic Committee refused to reinstate me. The old Jim Ryun wanted to express his anger to each committee member with a swift kick from my size 12 track shoe, but I knew the new Jim Ryun couldn't respond that way."

Though he lost the race, he had won in something much more important—a life-changing relationship that proved itself real in the middle of the most frustrating circumstances. He started using his notoriety as a platform to share his faith—even sponsoring and participating in road races for the opportunity to address the runners afterward and tell them about Christ.

He also did something that he advises every Christian to do—famous or not—as a tool for sharing their faith. He developed a personal tract that tells his story, together with the simple biblical steps by which anyone can enter into a personal relationship with Christ. "When you talk to people who are interested in something more, you can't always share at that moment, but you have something to give them that they can read later. It's a good way to present the gospel in a non-obtrusive manner." And using a bit of creativity and the aid of a photocopier, anyone can have a personal message worth leaving when time allows for nothing more.

Consistent witnessing became a part of the Jim Ryun's lifestyle—talking about God was as natural as talking about running. It's all an integral part of who Jim Ryun is. "I know I'm not the person I would have been if I hadn't met Christ, so I want people to see that."

POINTS TO PONDER

1. If you developed a short tract about your life and experience with Christ, what life issues would you address?

2. Plan to sit down before the week is out and draw up a tract you could develop to share how Christ can be life's greatest answer.

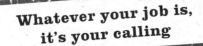

Whatever your job is, it's your calling

nd it should become an extension of who you are as a Christian. Whatever your job at this stage of your life, that is the opportunity or position God wants you to use as a vessel for Him. That comes in different forms. Many times your witness is the good work you do, the integrity you display being punctual as well as diligent n your work. I think people sometimes feel that when they become Christian, the place that they've got to go is to the pulpit. But each f us has our own individual pulpit by the uniqueness of the calling hat God has given us in our particular job. That's the race we'd better e running.

JIM RYUN
Kansas congressman

There is nothing so secular
that it cannot be sacred,
and that is one of deepest messages
of the Incarnation.

MADELEINE L'ENGLE

FINDING
THE POWER OF THE CALL

Graham Lacey, an international businessman and entrepreneur, a friend to England's royal family and to politicians and religious leaders throughout the world, has experienced the power of responding to God's call. In our interview, he gave us three critical steps for someone seeking that same power:

"First, find a spiritual mentor. Look for someone in your church you admire, someone who has what you'd like to have. Pray and then ask him/her to be your mentor. Tell him/her you want an accountability partner who will share personal experiences and spiritual wisdom to help you mature as a believer.

"The second thing I would do is study the laymen of New Testament Scripture. And be encouraged to see how God used very ordinary people who were sold out for Christ.

"Third, prayerfully claim through the power of the Holy Spirit that you would be given the strength, the insight, the direction, and the sensitivity to be sold out for Christ."

hrough Graham's long and remarkable career, he's gained nsight into the importance of being called into the marketplace.

"It would have been easy for me to serve the Lord full-time because I love the Word. But for me, that would be opting out because the harder thing is to be a called businessman confronted with all the issues and pressures to compromise ethically and morally. I think the pressure of being in business makes me more effective as a believer. I have credibility to reach the people who've made it, but who are spiritually hungry.

"If God wrote it on the wall today, I'd go full-time and preach the Gospel. Believe me, there were many times I would have chosen to do that. But I've chosen a different path because I'm convinced that it's my call. I'm convinced of that because every time I think of going to the 'greener pastures' of preaching, somebody enters my life with whom I have a chance to share Christ, usually someone the traditional church wouldn't be able to reach. Because that continues to happen, I know that I'm right where I'm supposed to be."

POINTS TO PONDER

1. Who is a mature Christian you could request to serve as a mentor in your life for the next several months?

2. What would you want to learn from him or her?

3. What are you waiting for?

'I FOUND IT'

Pat MacMillan joined forces with Bruce Cook, a Harvar MBA who had also found Christ, Dr. Howard Hendricks of Dalla Theological Seminary, and several other exectutives to launch a ministr called Leadership Dynamics. Their first consulting assignment wa for the national *I Found It* campaign sponsored by Campus Crusad The major media campaign featured ads with the tease "I Found It causing people to wonder what had been found and why "it" was s important. The "it," of course, was a personal relationship with Chris Tens of thousands "found" Christ through this campaign.

On the heels of this success, Pat launched his own consulting firr called Team Resources. Believing that the Bible was the be business book ever written, Pat developed outstanding leadershi materials focusing on team development, conflict management, an other leadership skills. His dream was to share what he'd learne with churches and ministries, but too often he found that they wer slow to take advantage of the Bible-based materials. Yet, whe business people heard Pat speak, they quickly invited him to teac his amazing *new* leadership material to their secular companies. Many were surprised that they had never heard this information before. Soon, Pat was consulting with Fortune 500 companies like Procter & Gamble, Campbell's Soup, Helene Curtis, L'Oreal, Bayer Aspirin, and Ocean Spray, providing what they considered to be highly effective management training—training that had its roots firmly planted in biblical principles.

"What was most amazing," reports Pat, "was that the ministries then started looking at us and saying, 'My goodness, these models worked for Fortune 500 companies, maybe they'll work as training models for us in ministry as well!' I couldn't believe it. It was almost like they had to see it work in the marketplace before they felt it would work in the church. All along my one prayer had been that this would make a difference in the church and ministries throughout North America—but God used the most amazing route to get me there. I would never have expected it.

"The further I went the more amazed I became at how God was leading my direction and my path. Years ago, Dr. Hendricks frequently shared with me, 'Pat, you know God's calling is not just a flash of insight, but, rather an unfolding like the unrolling of a blueprint.'"

And so it is. God's will unfolds to us sequentially, step by step, leading exactly where He wants us to go. Psalm 32:8 gives an amazing sense of security when He promises, "I will instruct you and teach you in the way you should go; I will guide you with My eye" (NKJV).

EXISTING
IN TWO DIMENSIONS

Jesus had a way of putting His finger on things that really matter. In just a few words, He would cut through the superfluous "fluff" of our existence and penetrate to the motives of the listener's heart. His goal was not simply to produce a big band of followers—but rather to produce deep-thinking, transformed followers who go beyond the superficial. He wanted followers who would live on two planes: the vertical and the horizontal. That's why, when Jesus was asked one of the most searching questions of all time—*What is the greatest commandment of all?*—He responded with the core essentials for depth and balance in healthy and dynamic living:

"Love the Lord your God with all your heart and with all your soul and with all your mind. This is the first and greatest commandment. And the second is like it: 'Love your neighbor as yourself.' All the Law and the Prophets hang on these two commandments (Matthew 22:37–40, NIV).

Jesus acknowledged that all of us coexist in both dimensions. He came to bring people into a right vertical relationship with our Creator so that we can function well horizontally with the people we live with every day.

John Calvin spoke of these two dimensions as the *primary* call and the *secondary* call. According to Calvin, the primary call is to enter a relationship with God. The secondary call is to a particular work, occupation, or vocation in life.

Churches are filled with good people who live nice lives but who fail to have a personal relationship with the One Who designed them. Their lives are unobtrusive, but God intended more. From the beginning of creation, God intended to enter into a personal and intimate relationship with His highest creation—us! When we go through the motions without any of the meaning, all we have is empty religious ritual. Jesus made sure to communicate that He would never be satisfied with that kind of insipid existence—nor should we. He declared, "I came that (you) may have and enjoy life, and have it in abundance—to the full, till it overflows" (John 10:10, AMP).

According to the Bible, we exist for the purpose of bringing others into a personal relationship with the Creator. The primary person we must please is the One who created us. When we do that, life will be an exciting ride!

THE CHOICE
IS OURS

"**Be strong and very courageous.** Obey all the laws Moses gave you. Do not turn away from them, and you will be successful in everything you do. Study this Book of the Law continually. Meditate on it day and night so you may be sure to obey all that is written in it. *Only then will you succeed*" (Joshua 1:7–8, NLT, italics ours).

The word for *success* in this passage in the original language means the "ability to make wise and prudent decisions"—which is the ultimate key to following God's call and will. The danger in losing sight of the principles of God that are found in His Word and forgetting how important they are to our everyday living is that we can drift away from our commitment to Him. We may turn from our devotion and obedience. And the warning needs to be heeded. Moses warned the people of Israel how critical this issue is when he said:

Now listen! Today I am giving you a choice between prosperity and disaster, between life and death. I have commanded you today to love the LORD your God and to keep his commandments, laws and regulations by walking in his ways. *If* you do this, you will live and become a great nation, and the LORD your God will bless you and the land you are about to enter and occupy. *But* if your heart turns away and you refuse to listen, and you if are drawn away to serve and worship other gods, *then* I warn you now that you will certainly be destroyed (Deuteronomy 30:15–18, NLT, italics ours).

God is clear that the choice is ours concerning what we do with His principles. We can choose to keep them centered and focused in our life, or we can drift from them and pay the consequences.

THE RIGHT
QUESTION

Henry Blackaby makes a great statement concerning God's personal will for our lives when he writes:

> "*What is God's will for my life?*—is *not* the right question. I think the right question is, *What is God's will?* Once I know God's will, then I can adjust my life to Him. In other words, what is it that God is purposing where I am? Once I know what God is doing, then I know what I need to do. The focus needs to be on *God*, not *my life!*" [4]

Throughout Scripture the key to daily, personal guidance from God was always maintaining an intimate relationship with Him. And it hasn't changed.

Wouldn't it be great if each of us had a huge spotlight...

. . that would reveal the years along our future path? It could illuminate every decision we face and the right or wrong steps to take. Unfortunately, life on our own doesn't work that way. As a result we trip and fall, get disoriented and lost, make wrong turns and—in general—leave a lot to be desired when we try to live life in our own wisdom.

God, on the other hand, sees far beyond even the spotlight we wish for. He knows the end from the beginning and has the big picture in perfect perspective. He sees the future as clearly as He sees the present, and He is willing to forgive the past to redeem the present.

To *commit* our way to the Lord literally means to roll our concerns, desires, and future into the Lord's hands. And the attitude that is required in the heart is the words of the old hymn, "*Wherever* He leads, I'll go." When we have a relationship based on obedience and trust in the One who created and called us to a plan and purpose, we inevitably find He can take care of us better than we can.

A PROMISE
WORTH LIVING FOR

God promises that if we obediently live by His principle when we're facing major choices, He will guide us in the right decision as we follow and fulfill His calling. His promise resonate in our heart when He says, "Your ears shall hear a word behind you saying, 'This is the way, walk in it,' whenever you turn to the right hand or whenever you turn to the left" (Isaiah 30:21, NKJV).

And He will guide our very steps. Just think on this promise:

"The steps of a [good] man are directed and established of the LORD when He delights in his way [and He busies Himself with his every step]. Though he falls, he shall not be utterly cast down, for the LORD grasps his hand in support and upholds him" (Psalm 37:23-24, AMP)

Now that's a promise worth living for!

"**God saved you by his special favor** when you believed. And you can't take credit for this; it was a gift from God. Salvation is not a reward for the good things we have done so none of us can boast about it. *For we are God's masterpiece. He has created us anew in Christ Jesus, so that we can do the good things he planned for us long ago*" (Ephesians 2:8–10, NCV italics ours).

Notice the word *masterpiece*. It's a great translation from the original language, which means a "work of art." That's exactly what you are in God's eyes. And He wants to do all the things in your life that Paul prayed for the Ephesians so that you can fulfill the "good things He planned for us long ago."

Sometimes Christians believe that, "If I lived in a different place or lived under different conditions, then I'd be a much better follower of Christ." We long for foreign mission fields or other challenging locations, picturing ourselves as a bold witness under extreme circumstances.

But God wants us to live in the here and now! He is not nearly as concerned with *where* and *what* as He is with *how*. The emphasis is not on the place you're doing something, the conditions under which you're doing it, or the role you are filling. Jesus is focused on how you're doing what you're doing right where you are.

To Do:
Be God's

GOD HAS MADE US WHAT WE ARE.
IN CHRIST JESUS,
GOD MADE US TO DO
GOOD WORKS,
WHICH GOD PLANNED IN ADVANCE FOR US
TO LIVE OUR LIVES DOING.

EPHESIANS 2:10 (NCV)

———✦———

THERE IS NO WORK BETTER THAN ANOTHER TO
PLEASE GOD.
TO WASH DISHES AND TO PREACH
ARE ALL ONE.

WILLIAM TYNDALE

———✦———

ARE YOU
FAT?

God is looking for FAT people—

> **Faithful**
>
> **Available**
>
> **Teachable**

When you're faithful, you're on time to work, you meet your deadline and you give more than is expected. Are you being faithful?

How about available? That means being open to new opportunitie . . . and willing to get out of your comfort zone. You're available righ where you are to help others, understanding that nobody's job i done until everybody's job is done.

You are teachable if you're willing to ask for help when you don know something. You have a goal to be a lifelong learner. If you'r teachable, you already have a mentor. And you're asking God t prepare you to be a mentor.

be FAT right where you are! And if you're thinking, *But you don't know my boss!*—God does. Or *My job is boring!*—maybe that's because you haven't invited God into the mix. Or if you think, *I just need a new opportunity.*—What about the opportunity you already have that you aren't faithfully fulfilling? No matter how small that opportunity might be, Jesus made it clear that He would look for those who are faithful in the little things; those are the ones He will honor with greater things.

How are you doing?

THE
ANSWER WE NEED

Jesus gave great counsel early in His ministry when He stood on the mount and declared to His followers:

> "Ask and it will be given to you; seek and you will find; knock and it will be opened to you. For everyone who asks receives, and he who seeks finds, and to him who knocks, it will be opened" (Matthew 7:7–8, NKJV).

When you read those verses in the original language, you discover that Jesus is talking about *persistent* asking, *continuous* seeking, and *relentless* knocking. In other words, Christ is telling us to be a heavenly pest! We are to be that small child in the backseat of the car with his "Are we there yet?" questions. You must do everything in your power to know and understand His will. He wants you to persevere, to finish what you begin—especially in asking and searching for the clarity of call and the direction of His plan.

What an amazing promise He gives for those who do just that—the promise that He inevitably will answer! In the Old Testament, God guaranteed, "Call to me and I will answer you and tell you great and unsearchable things you do not know" (Jeremiah 33:3, NIV).

Notice there is no "maybe" or "sometimes" either in this Old Testament promise or from Christ's promise in the Sermon on the Mount. God will *always* answer. He doesn't promise that He will always give the answer we *want* to hear, but He does promise to *always* answer and show us what we *need* to hear.

THEN
GET IN!

Years ago a French aerialist by the name of Charles Blondin was the first man to walk the tightrope across Niagara Falls. Having seen an aerialist as a small child, Blondin set his mind on becoming the best in the world. By the time he was eight, he was dubbed "The Little Wonder." And year after year he only got better.

In 1858 he saw Niagara Falls for the first time. He decided then that he would be the first aerialist to conquer the Falls.

On June 30, 1859, before a mesmerized crowd, Blondin stretched a three-inch hemp cord across the raging river, right above the Falls. At one end it towered 160 feet high. At the other end it was 270 feet above the ground. He crossed with ease and became an immediate legend.

Blondin returned numerous times to cross the surging waters in a variety of ways. One time he balanced a chair midway across and then stood on the chair. He crossed the river on a bicycle, on stilts, in a sack, and once he crossed blindfolded! One of his most popular feats was to take a small stove, stop part-way, cook breakfast, and then lower it to cheering passengers on the tour boat below.

In September 1860, the Prince of Wales was in the audience. That day Blondin carried his manager piggyback across Niagara Falls. The prince was amazed but begged Blondin not to do it again. With a mischievous grin, Blondin asked if the Prince believed he could push the prince himself across the Falls in a wheelbarrow.

"Sure," the prince replied.

Before he could say another word, Blondin commanded, "Then get in!"

The last time anyone saw the prince that day, he was scrambling away from the Falls as fast as he could!

Do we sometimes respond in the same way to God? He asks, "Do you think I can successfully guide your steps and order your life?" And we say, "Sure!" But when He says "Then get in," we start backtracking. He asks us to do something outrageous and exciting, and we start walking away from the Falls. Could it be we are really saying, "I believe you can guide my steps, *as long as it makes sense to me*. But there are more choices out there, and I want to keep my options open."

The bottom line is we either trust God or we don't. We're either willing to be obedient or we leave our options open. Yet He continually invites us on the ride of our lives!

So the choice is up to you. Are you willing to "get in the wheel-barrow" and trust God? And even if you don't know where the future is leading, and even if it sometimes seems "insane," are you willing to follow God with radical obedience? If so, we promise it will be the ride of your life!

SEEKING
WISE COUNSEL

God loves us enough to send mature, seasoned, and integrity-filled believers into our lives. We watch them model wisdom and godly living. We start to think, "The further I go on my journey, the more I want to become like _____."

We watch them in their walk with God and those around them, and we see firsthand the impact they make. It doesn't take us long to determine that we want to have vertical and horizontal relationships and influence like they do.

We want to encourage you to seek some wise counsel from that person; but first, a warning. They may be godly, but they are not God. Like all of us, they have a sin nature and they are only one step away from disobedience. If they are truly godly, they would be the first to tell you not to put your faith in them. Put your faith in Christ. Look to others for counsel, but not for salvation. Men and women will disappoint; only Christ is perfectly faithful.

Once you find a godly man or woman who represents the kind of Christian you would like to become, set up a lunch, dinner, or coffee at Starbucks with them. Tell them you're looking for some counsel and a sounding board as you seek to hear God's call on your life and to fulfill His plan for the future. Be ready with some questions that will help you learn from their journey such as:

How did you personally discover God's call and plan for your life?

How did you discover your passion, and how did that tie in with God's call?

What are some ways God helped you "hear" His call on your life and understand His plan for your future?

Was it a sudden experience or was it an unfolding journey?

How did God use your temperament, talents, spiritual giftedness, and experiences to reveal His call and plan?

What would you do differently if you were going through the journey all over again?

It's also incredibly helpful to read some of the autobiographies and biographies of great Christian leaders who God has called and through whom God has made a significant difference. Almost without exception you will find them talking about God's call on their life and the unveiling of His plan for coming alongside Him in mission.

Rely first and foremost on Scripture. But don't be afraid to read other stories that will inspire you and other resources that will help make life count. If you're going to make an impact, you've got to be a reader. Learn from the experiences of others. Many great books are available that will help you immensely on this journey.

Years ago, our friend Bill Bright, founder of Campus Crusade for Christ, wrote *The Four Spiritual Laws*, a booklet that gained worldwide popularity. In it there is a simple yet profound diagram of a train.

Notice that the steam engine is labeled *Fact* (as in God's declared Word), the coal car is labeled *Faith*, and the caboose is labeled *Feelings*. In a train like this, it doesn't matter whether the caboose stays hooked on or disconnected—if there's coal in the steam engine, the train will run. In the same way, when we put our faith in God's declared Word, regardless of our feelings, the train runs. And the amazing thing is this: when we do so, our feelings begin to follow our faith.

BE ANXIOUS FOR NOTHING, BUT IN EVERYTHING BY PRAYER AND SUPPLICATION, **WITH THANKSGIVING,** LET YOUR REQUESTS BE MADE KNOWN TO GOD; AND THE PEACE OF GOD, WHICH SURPASSES ALL UNDERSTANDING, WILL GUARD YOUR HEARTS AND MINDS THROUGH CHRIST JESUS.

PHILIPPIANS 4:6-7 (NKJV)

THE SECRET OF CHRISTIANITY IS NOT DOING, THE SECRET IS **"BEING."** IT IS BEING THE POSSESSOR OF THE **NATURE OF CHRIST.**

JOHN G. LAKE

YOU HAVE A CALL
...BE WILLING TO HEAR IT

The amazing thing about God's will is that He wants us to know it sometimes more than we want to discover it. And He makes us this promise: if we have a willing ear, we will clearly hear His voice.

When Paul had a radical encounter with Jesus Christ on the road to Damascus, he was struck blind. Three days later Ananias was sent by God to give Paul a word about his ability to know God's will. Ananias declared,

"The God of our forefathers has destined and appointed you to come progressively to know His will—that is, to perceive, to recognize more strongly and clearly and to become better and more intimately acquainted with His will" (Acts 22:14, AMP).

But even at such defining moments, everything is not automatic. As T. B. Maston said years ago:

> The call to follow Him is not only His initial invitation, but, since none of us follows Him as closely or perfectly as we should, it is also His continuing call or invitation. As we respond to this invitation of Jesus, we shall discover that it has much more depth and meaning than we had anticipated. We shall discover that it affects every area of our lives. We shall come to comprehend more fully that it means to walk in the way that Jesus Himself walked, which was in complete obedience to the will of the Father. Here is enough to challenge us to the end of life's journey![5]

Maston is so right—it's a lifelong journey. But like all journeys, it starts with a single step. In this case the step is clear. The very first step in discovering God's will for your life is to really desire to know it with all your heart.

Why don't you just stop and pray that God will give you a burning passion to know and do His will for your life?

WITH GOD'S POWER

WORKING IN US, GOD CAN DO MUCH, MUCH MORE

THAN ANYTHING

WE CAN ASK OR IMAGINE.

TO HIM BE

GLORY

IN THE CHURCH AND IN

CHRIST JESUS

FOR ALL TIME, FOREVER AND EVER.

AMEN.

EPHESIANS 3:20-21 (NCV)

BENEDICTION

So I bow in prayer before the Father from
whom every family in heaven and on earth gets its
true name. I ask the Father in his great glory to
give you the power to be strong inwardly through
his Spirit. I pray that Christ will live in your hearts
by faith and that your life will be strong in love and
be built on love. And I pray that you and all God's
holy people will have the power to understand the
greatness of Christ's love—how wide and how long
and how high and how deep that love is. Christ's
love is greater than anyone can ever know, but I
pray that you will be able to know that love. Then
you can be filled with the fullness of God.

EPHESIANS 3:14-19 (NCV)

Endnotes

1. J.I. Packer, *A Quest for Godliness* (Wheaton, Ill.: Crossway Books, 1990), pp. 23, 24.

2. Findley Edge, *The Doctrine of the Laity* (Nashville: Convention Press, 1985).

3. Charles Swindoll, *The Mystery of God's Will* (Nashville: W Publishing Group, 1999), p. 181.

4. Henry Blackaby and Claude King, *Experiencing God* (Nashville: LifeWay Press, 1990), p. 14.

5. T. B. Maston, *God's Will and Your Life* (Nashville: Broadman Press, 1964), p. 10.

CONTINUING
THE JOURNEY

Made to Count:
Discovering What to Do with Your Life

A call to the secular marketplace, or to work in the home, is just as significant as a call to the ministry! Using eight powerful biblical principles, as well as the fascinating stories of people changed by them, Bob Reccord and Randy Singer teach you how to hear God's call and discover His specific plan for you. These principles transcend time, cultures, and occupations. They are broadly universal and, yet, individually unique. This book can change your life . . . then you can change your world. Read it now and discover the potential you have to make a significant difference in the world—how you have been divinely made to count.

Made to Count Life Planner:
A Six-Week Plan for Finding Your Calling
and Discovering What to Do with Your Life

(coming in November 2004)

Filled with interactive exercises and probing questions, The Made to Count Life Planner takes readers on a journey to discover their own calling in life.

Made to Count Group Study Kit

(coming in November 2004)